THIS SCEPTRED ISLE

GW00598841

Jane A. M. Hayes

ARTHUR H. STOCKWELL LTD.
Elms Court   Ilfracombe   Devon
Established 1898

British Library Cataloguing-in-Publication Data.
A catalogue record for this book is available
from the British Library.

By the same author:
An Anthology for Everyone
Light of Shalom
A Portrait of London
The Seasons
This Savage Paradise

ISBN 0 7223 3018-9

Printed in Great Britain by
Arthur H. Stockwell Ltd.
Elms Court   Ilfracombe
Devon

Introduction

It would be difficult to argue that England may be counted as other than one of the most delightful countries in the world that it is my privilege therefore to write about the many places which both dazzle and delight the senses and intellect, for like a great tapestry, the land unfolds not only in its architectural splendour but in the landscape also which is as divine as it is charming and as soothing as it is spectacular! The luscious green of fields and meadows is a balm that if we were to live to be a hundred, life might still be counted too short, depriving us of that foretaste of delights we anticipate in the afterlife!

In this short volume of verse, I have taken you with me from places as far apart as Oban in Scotland to Maritime Portsmouth on the South coast, lingering somewhat in our capital City of London to savour the majestic wonders of buildings closely associated with great State events and ceremonies. (I myself live in the house where Jennie Churchill once dwelt and near the house where once resided Dame Nellie Melba and situated in the same road where Charles Dickens too rented an apartment where he wrote much of *"Edwin Drood"*.) I have also included verse about the quaint villages and towns which offer the surprises we love and have loved from the days of childhood to our more mature years.

Our aesthetic appetite is well catered for as well as those more eccentric tastes (so English). Brighton Pavilion must be the most outstanding example of the latter whilst the City of Bath is notable for appealing to the former with its elegant splendour and restrained refinement. (Small wonder that so many great artists have been inspired by such varied wonders and certainly for those who find solace in portraying the landscape, the choice is rich indeed!)

As well as seeing our heritage in the places I have already mentioned, we are reminded of our musical genius in the music of William Byrd as well as Elgar about whom I have written at some length and concerts too may be heard at Kenwood House. (I have written one poem about this beautiful place.) Marble Hill House, Audley End House and West Park House form the backdrop to musical evenings where these may be heard out of doors. (How can anyone resist Delius's Summer Night On The River when performed by the lake at Kenwood House that it really does not require me to state the obvious when a feast of music may be heard in such a magical setting!)

Having now set out my own thoughts however briefly on the subject of the many wonders of our Island Country, it now only remains for me to hope that you may find the time to dip into this little book and share with me the pleasure of recalling or anticipating the enjoyment derived from seeing some of the many treasures which England boasts since so much represents our heritage of which we may be justly proud. Let us trust therefore that our children and grandchildren may continue to sustain these wonders since our historic past is one which we may be proud to admit hoping always that future generations may learn to respect their heritage as much as we all pray that more may be added in the years which lie ahead.

J.H.

Preface

Man sets his hand against the flinty rock
And overturns mountains by the roots.
He carves out channels through the rock;
His eyes behold every precious thing.
He dams up the sources of the streams
So that hidden things may be brought to light.

Kethuvim
JOB Chapter 28
Verses: 9—12

Contents

List of Illustrations

Résumé

Our nation's heritage, this our glory,
Towns and cities tell a story,
Queen of West, Bath surprises
From honey-coloured streets, the Crescent rises;
A Georgian City, Western candy,
Recall Beau Brummell, Regency dandy!
And Roman Baths unearthed spell history,
Since revealed, conceal they mystery,
Contrasted Pump Rooms, recent past,
Giving present, reason last;
Found Avon County, see hot springs,
Nature's wonders, hear bells ring!

       And Shakespeare's birthplace, this a treat,
       Location found at Henley Street,
       A market town, busy, bustling,
       With Hathaway's spectre nearby rustling;
       Anne the loved one, she bard's wife,
       Thus inspired, plays came to life
       Near Stratford Theatre, this world famed,
       Called the Memorial, aptly named!
       Close to river where swans glide,
       See peaceful scene, no thought deride,
       Where England's greatness is enshrined
       Midst mellow buildings, all entwined!

But go now south to Portsmouth Town,
With naval base found no cause frown,
Where docked the *Victory* and *Mary Rose*,
Great exhibits, questions pose;
How achieved such conservation,
Warships these, no reservation,
How history made in different age,
That marvel all both young and sage;
Ask how in past such ships were made,
Withstand a foe, dare England raid?
Flagships sturdy, both seen fight,
Demonstrating they Great Britain's might!

And inland Warwick springs to mind,
Place historic, manors find
With Newbold Revel, little known,
Near Monk's Kirby, stands alone;
Once a hub of country life,
Neglected culture, with time the scythe,
Where industry here has taken toll,
Seen populace dwindle, smaller roll,
Though all that has been lingers still,
As village squire finds time may fill;
But green and pleasant lies the land,
Leafy still with memories grand!

But more remote the Scottish Isles,
Five hundred number, miles and miles,
Where hardy folk dwell, desolate spot,
Loving land all, bless their lot,
On Isles of Raasay, Eigg and Mull,
Where Oban nearby, dreams may lull,
Since far away the madding crowd,
Gives no chance here fears may cloud,
For peace here found with some respite,
Feel calm serenity, easing fright,
As place here ponder, meditate,
With no cause hasten destiny's fate!

Elizabeth Regina

The principle of Monarchy, Head of State,
Lady gracious, steadfast, great,
For awesome task to wear the Crown,
A heavy weight n'er borne with frown;
A supreme symbol, dazzles the mind
That hard imagine equal find,
For great the burden, marking reign,
Lasting lifetime, nought seen feign,
Since steadfast Queen and one beloved
Who men admire, all above,
As through the ages, eras marked,
The Monarch's nature shown embarked,
Encouraging a future approved from throne
So stamp our greatness, n'er atone,
As by the nation nought disregarded,
Honoured Monarch, high regarded,
When time of war 'gainst the foe
Men gave their lives, saved land from woe!
Thus past survived fight other days
For none e'er weakened, showing way,
How lead others, ideals n'er torn,
Showing nation, those unborn,
The way gained greatness, ages past,
Thus paved a future, one to last,
For men of hour found, witness war
When Queen's late father showed the door
To transgressor, evil known,
So let children mature, all grown,
Taught love their country, Monarch too,
Learn both love, remaining true;
Faithful, loyal, proving strong,
So lead their lives, men trust these long!
For slow our recovery, deprivation,
As war incurred much privation,
That maintain struggle, King inspired
Strong sense of duty, helped aspire,
Lives enriched by freedom won,
Led rejoicing, when tyrant gone!
Reason awe, way Queen revered,
Our fealty known, this all adhere,

With ideals fused so lead the world,
Men understanding, flags unfurl,
As united, all are proud,
State all equal, thought n'er cloud
The nation's rights, men respect,
Notion known, each expects,
Forge ideals, these Monarch's aims,
Glad that others share same claim,
That united, peace all seek
As in friendship, none known meek,
Binding ties and understanding
For no room here, misunderstanding,
Engendered pattern, set by Queen,
Hence proud the nation, Monarch seen
Men at work and may have talked
As she midst people, midst them walked,
Showing all how much she cares
For her peoples and may share
Ideals common, proud obey,
That honour Monarch, please each day!

Leeds Castle

Listed in the Domesday Book,
Today see ancient Castle Leeds,
Most romantic in the Kingdom
Where history speaks of noble deeds!
For famous once as Norman stronghold,
Royal residence to medieval Queens,
And playground to Henry VIII
Our crowning glory, glad all seen
In historic setting with famous gardens,
There view islands on the lake,
Surrounded by a green arc parkland,
Such memories of trees and hills we take,
All tumbling gently there to water,
Find glorious views once seen by Kings,
English beauty lasting all the year,
Doubtless heard, the bluebells ring!
Administered all by Leeds Foundation,
All now found with love restored,
For within the Castle many treasures,
Where medieval furnishings find adored!

Enchanting Castle, English beauty,
Enduring long o'er many years,
Though seasons change, n'er the Castle
For history tells us nought here fear!
Built in stone by Norman Barons
All nine hundred years ago,
Fortified, enlarged, enriched,
Sturdy built, withstand the foe!
Conveyed to Crown, least three centuries,
Where love and romance once were known,
All much loved by successive Kings,
Celebrated Monarchs, Castle owned!
Saved for nation by Lady Baillie
Who established a Foundation on her death,
Thus Park and Castle all preserved
Before the Lady took last breath!
Acquired for enjoyment of the public,
Mainly in pursuit of peace,
And advancement of research,
Promoting art, great works released!

Concerts too at Leeds are held,
All in keeping, past preserved,
That these attractions, much beloved
By a nation who deserved
This attention, strong reminder
How with love the past restored,
Seeing history all around,
Paintings, tapestries, all adored
With works of art all on display,
Present meets those lives long past,
Happy ghosts, they many lurking,
Where Leeds Castle, legends last:
As all may feel too leaves breathe history,
Sense this walking in the grounds,
Once a palace to Henry VIII
Who all sense still makes the rounds!
For crowning glory here is setting,
Where seen woods and waterfalls,
Viewed from Castle, glorious vision,
Place nought shrouded and time n'er palls!

Leeds Castle   The Aviary

The spectacular modern aviary was opened by H.R.H. Princess Alexander, Royal Patron of Leeds Castle Foundation, in 1988. It houses a collection of more than 100 rare species of bird and aims not only to be a focal point of conservation, but also at successful breeding — to reintroduce endangered species into their original habitat.

The Royal Pavilion Brighton

The Royal Pavilion, magic world,
Decorated in the Chinese taste,
Brighton home to three great Monarchs,
So much here, see no time waste!
With Regency Palace, this breathtaking,
A Farmhouse once transformed by Nash,
With Indian exterior, seen alluring,
At Brighton seaside, cutting dash!
First built there for George IV
When was used by younger brother,
William known as Sailor King,
Who both loved place as each to other!
Its architect was Henry Holland
Who built the villa on the site,
Which Nash transformed to present Palace,
Echoing ever Regal might!
For inside seen a fantasy world,
With mythical creatures, none found mean,
Where furnishings there seem all so fanciful,
On loan today from present Queen!

Witness extravagant Music Room,
With domed ceiling of scallop shaped shells,
Then walk length of the Long Gallery,
All bright coloured, imagine bells,
Peeling they, sounds rejoicing
In a riot of imagined sounds,
Recalls those concerts, long forgotten,
Hear all, see all, make the rounds!
And see the kitchen with cast-iron palm trees
Where is placed the copperware,
For food once served in Banqueting Room,
That ease imagine, all who dare,
The clock set back to Georgian times,
Seeing chandelier dominate,
Held in place by silver dragon,
Such a marvel, hard relate,
Find Drawing Room with quiet grace,
Private rooms all showing charm,
They all seen on upper floor,
That back in time step, no alarm!

The Royal Pavilion   Brighton

For Queen Victoria, once there dwelt,
That wonder Albert, what he thought,
When all far cry, from plainer castles,
That dare we wonder, dare we ought!
Though bracing sea air, main attraction
Must have brought the Prince Consort
There to visit, examine treasures
When couple braved the Royal Resort!
For known extraordinary this quaint Palace,
Europe elsewhere, the like not seen,
With these fantasies, unimagined,
As elsewhere no such culture keen!
That reason today we brave Pavilion,
Discover copies of finest prints,
Ceramics too with many fabrics,
Seen gifts many, nothing stint!
For great attraction, Royal Pavilion,
Drawing crowds, exploring place,
Once the home to British Monarchs
Who from Palace, ocean faced!

Fine naval flagship, the *Victory* stands,
At Maritime Portsmouth, British land,
Where plaque marks spot where Nelson died,
As seen red boards, red blood tried hide!
Disguising horror of the fight,
So shroud death from sailors' sight;
Though must have known, those men who fought,
How great price paid when battle bought,
Great price history paid which lingers still,
That no doubt great deeds here fulfilled
When famous words, these known all time,
'England expects from men all fine,
To do their duty, time of war,
And show a tyrant England's door!'

See in the Dockyard, *Mary Rose*,
Ship raised to surface, wonders pose
As artefacts seen they, these not few
In conservation workshop, where may view
Historic vessel, Henry's pride,
As back in time step, nought deride,
As craftsmen study ancient ship,
A sturdy craft built, n'er left drift,
But part convoy and one to fight,
Proving ever Britain's might,
Precursor those in 1588
Which fought Armada, nought berate,
When smaller vessels, order Queen,
Lent Drake's name to posterity keen!

As seen at Portsmouth, coastline view,
Feel fresh breezes, not a few,
Play 'gainst cliffs, known o'er the years,
With safe harbour, see jutting pier,
Where ferry too from Gosport lends,
A pleasant means reach journey's end,
Those with wish to see birthplace
Where Dickens first came face to face
With world unknown 'cept Victorian times
And learned of life in English clime,
How social ills these did abound
As he from Portsmouth looked around,
Leaving he, childhood retreat
To savour meanness, London's streets!

Place Havant, Cosham too form scheme,
English landscape, Portsmouth's dream,
Suburbs all to dockland life,
Find place to rest, retire from strife;
For time of war here known through ages,
Where history relays all those pages
Of naval legends once began,
They o'er centuries, covered span,
Documenting they so many deeds,
Enacted all with greatest speed,
So save a nation, rescue race,
One n'er known to e'er lose face
When back 'gainst wall, time peril known,
Where maritime cunning, there had grown!

For special place this, southern coast,
With Isle of Wight near, place to boast,
And Hayling Island, this a gem
On English Channel, diadem!
Such place to love, revere, adore,
Where waves come lapping on the shore,
For who can argue 'gainst such landscape
As cliffs men pass to fields escape,
There where orchards offer shade,
'Neath trees with fruit of highest grade,
Offering succour, some respite,
With calmer air, less breeze despite
Closeness they to gusty scene,
Makes Portsmouth Harbour, proud we've been!

Buckingham Palace

Official residence of the Queen,
Glad all those, glad have seen
Priceless treasures therein housed,
All admire, where awe aroused;
Viewing porcelain, paintings, lovely rooms,
All so many, dispelling gloom,
Seeing statues, clocks ornate,
All so many, hard relate,
Such rich variety, lovely art,
That where begin, ask where start?
So much outstanding, leaves bereft,
Speechless mortals, pondering depth,
Thoughts too deep, all inspired,
Every item need inquire
Their past history, ask where begin
As in hushed silence, heard no din,
For heavy quiet reigns o'er all.
Solemn splendour casts a pall,
As we gaze, all in wonder,
So much beauty, Palace ponder!

For Duke of Buckingham once owned home,
A name recall as Palace roam,
Until George III, he moved there,
Bought the house and did share
Stately house with his Queen,
Consort Charlotte, there once seen,
Until William IV came to the throne,
Commissioned architect, added stone,
For past omissions, found too small,
Such a house, home to all,
Monarch's staff and noble Lords,
In attendance, could afford,
Build State Palace, seen today,
Fitting home for Royalty,
Thus John Nash was employed,
His great genius, thus deployed,
Added to building, adding back,
For no expense spared, none did lack,
Created Palace, fit for King,
For posterity allowed splendour cling!

Buckingham Palace

Thus Royal Patron and John Nash,
Improved the Palace, added dash,
Unrivalled splendour before n'er seen,
For Sovereign next indeed was Queen,
When Victoria it was who ascended throne,
With growing family, added stone,
Built the East Wing, Edward Blore,
He the architect, added more,
Enlarged the Palace, joining wings,
By closing forecourt, planned privacy bring,
For once too public, Royal home,
Prepared for future, Queen alone,
Since private life, she preferred,
Family sanctum, crowds deferred,
For Queen Victoria, family life,
All too public, such made strife,
That Queen's seclusion, thus respected,
And courtiers too, they expected
That Palace splendour guard their lives,
From public scrutiny, aid Royalty survive!

Elgar

Elgar, he above all others
Through his music portrays the land,
A proud people, sturdy stock,
We known slow accept new brand,
Reflect a culture, this our own,
For no mistake we wish outshine
Those, all others, neighbours ours,
Express desire hear music fine;
That when discovered, artist ours,
No mistake we glad rejoice,
Hearing sounds, reflect our nature,
Gives men reason praise with voice,
Adding too great tolling bells,
Enshrining thus such rare event,
Means by which men may reflect
The nation's psyche, sounds cement;
For thus our nature, British soul,
Adding colour to belief,
In our souls a dedication,
Gives outlet, allows relief!

But hard explain why we so tardy
Find such music in a man,
Musician speaking he for nation
In a language, classic span;
As sounds divine, heard choral works,
Symphonic structures too we hear,
With concertos these, all heard played,
Expressing thoughts too deep for tears,
Such lovely works thus men may share,
English soul expressed each line,
Reflect our greatness when souls bared,
Annual heard, count country fine,
Olympian greatness thus discovered
When men with courage reach great heights,
Grappling they portray sweet sounds,
Echoing English soul, the might,
And plumb the depths of English soul
Through great music, portray our kind,
We a nation, one to last,
For in art hear English mind!

Thus hear nation's greatness echo
Through a single man's resolve,
Portraying heart and mettle both
Through a seer's mind absolve,
As heard our faults all melded thus,
As men all strive to overcome
Through our music, sweet delight,
So forge aims and thus become
Determined all attain great heights
When Land of Hope and Glory sing,
This heard echoing round Albert Hall
As last night of proms heard ring!
When men with fervour so determine
Confirm a greatness nation savours
As past weeks a feast enjoyed,
Hearing music with this flavour,
Completes the cycle with resolve,
So vow next year all strive employ
Same resources, music's feast,
Preserve a heritage all enjoy!

Kenwood

Kenwood House, rural idyll,
Outstanding monument, nothing vanished,
A house so near, close to town,
Work of art, seen nothing banished,
As standing proud today at Hampstead,
An elegant home of classic hue
By Robert Adams, long remodelled,
Near London Town, boasts splendid view!
The Park designed by Humphry Repton,
This includes an ornamental lake
Midst fields and meadows, in such contrast,
We glad there City life forsake!
And in the house see Mansfield's Library,
Adam's masterpiece of renown,
Such achievement, all take pride
That find no cause here folk may frown,
With famed collection of many paintings
By Edward Guinness, all bequeathed,
The finest known in all the land
That view today find some relief;
With works by Turner, Gainsborough too
And many others, pride of place;
Portraits seen of long dead guests
When visit house, view face to face;
And Kenwood famed too for its concerts,
As the summer, heard sweet sounds,
Where many held there by the lake,
All so lovely in the grounds!
For nowhere else found such a setting,
Contrasts with the Heath below,
As with music, birds heard singing
Beside the lake which gently flows;
A place to meet and solace find,
Enjoyment seek with place to rest,
Where we walk there at our leisure,
Admiring landscape, this the best,
England's heritage, this the model,
With art and music, all combined,
See Kenwood House, sturdy, English,
Stand today, place pleasure find!

Kenwood

The Tower of London

The Tower of London, grey fortress,
Nine hundred years stands o'er the City,
Palace built 1078
Place where past known little pity!
Once State prison, harbouring traitors,
Where terror reigned 'til life's end
When heads were severed on the block
As lost souls then were made amend
All crimes known against the State,
King he exercising he his rights,
Horrid spot where lessons learned,
How Monarch there dislayed his might!
With prisoners past, Thomas More and Walter Raleigh,
(Both met end at different times)
Distinguished men these, greatness theirs,
Accused of treason, this their crime!
For times were harsh and Yeomen warders
Were entrusted guard the Tower gates,
The welfare too of famous prisoners,
Their task to guard 'til end relate!

    Legends here too, these abound
    Where enigmatic ravens in Tower found live,
    They in past fed severed heads
    That now to feed them, all fear give,
    When seen gathered in the place,
    Known times past, execution site,
    Where axe claimed head of Anne Boleyn,
    Lady Jane Grey too, birds alight!
    Reliving past, or so it seems,
    For hard forget these lives cut short,
    However noble, end came swift,
    Though today seems birds care nought
    For past spirits living on,
    That when seen ravens, dark tales tell,
    For mercy none shown any prisoner,
    That wonder Yeomen there who dwell,
    Seeing daily, grim reminders
    How ruthless men cared for Kings,
    Extorting they such sad confessions
    Afore from prisoners life did wring!

The Tower of London

A fortress in the City of London, on the River Thames: begun in 1078; later extended and used as a palace, the main State prison, and now as a museum containing the Crown Jewels.

Men tortured first that death came sweet,
For well known how the rack did stretch
Flesh and sinews, torn so cruel,
That screams for mercy, none cared fetch!
Spine chilling tales these, all so many
That rejoice when seen Crown Jewels contrast,
Show English best, this all displayed
With greatness shining, enhances past!
Makes an orgy, rich jewels brilliant,
History discovered behind grey walls,
Splendid, varied, much relate
That ask where start where nothing palls,
Seeing England's history here enshrined
Where every nook and cranny speaks,
Though place where only hardy souls dare walk,
Since this no site dare linger meek,
Place historians come research,
Marvel ever, much to ponder,
Such a past, England harbours
In the Tower place reason wonders!

The Saint's Way

Despite long years of Celtic tradition,
The lives of Cornish saints remain unknown,
None are named as in Dark Ages
That path known Saint's Way has o'ergrown;
Winding twenty miles across granite spine
Where Padstow linked on northern coast,
Inaugerated there ten years ago,
Today celebrates religious journey most,
From sandy expanse of Camel Estuary
Where Celtic missionaries same route walked
A path the same day, enjoyed by thousands,
Finding project few wish balk!
An inspired accident in parish of Luxulyan,
Where discovered remains of granite stiles,
That men suspected path once part of ancient route
Where Bronze Age travellers walked for miles!
Though exact route not yet been plotted
That evidence assembled conceived the Saint's Way,
When teams across Cornwall cleared the undergrowth,
Cutting steps, to form rights of way!

      Farmers helped too, moved obstructions,
      That folk now find path, this contrasts
      With lovely treasures, there discovered,
      That travellers remember all that lasts,
      For Saint's Way well known an enigma,
      Once guided pilgrims, helped o'erland,
      Hearing legends as they walked
      How men and dragons they held hands!
      Time when Petroc, known Welsh man's son,
      Famed he for the kindest acts,
      As to animals as well as folk,
      That reason doubt not this a fact!
      Once rescuing a stag from shooting party,
      Released sea monster trapped in lake,
      And removed a splinter from dragon's eye,
      That doubt not goodness nor forsake
      The memory of known greatest saint,
      Showing kindness, lasting fame,
      When Cornwall once a home for hermits,
      That remember all time we his name!

The Saint's Way

From its halfway point at the village of Lanivet, the Saint's Way rises to the awesome granite outcrop of Halman Tor. On a clear day, the view stretches 50 miles towards Dartmoor.

King Brychan of Wales too, an early traveller,
With him came as well more saints,
That apt find place this now so named,
Makes inappropriate argue travellers feint,
Place guarded all by cliffs of Pentire,
Where Camel Estuary retains power enchant,
Important haven for wading birds,
For serene woods here, men wish plant,
Home for curlews, men on high land,
Since wolves once prowled midst oak and ash,
No habitat dark woods, men sought shelter
Free from dangers, when safety dashed!
Though now on clear days, all view Dartmoor,
Whilst to south, path trails away,
Place china clay industry dominates land to west,
Encourages travellers return another day,
When see Luxulyan with buzzards circling
Though sense of peace felt overland,
Since privilege walk length of the Saint's Way,
Pilgrims constant, remain faithful band!

Blenheim Palace

Born at Blenheim Palace, Vanbrugh's house,
Sir Winston Churchill, man of fame,
House gift from nation, such a Palace,
Aft great battle, so gained name!
At Woodstock, Oxford, there is found,
Marvel all when seen this gift,
With the Maze and Pleasure Gardens,
Place inspires our souls uplift;
Refreshing all, feel close to heaven
Seeing tapestries, paintings, these all fine,
With Blenheim Library, such a niche,
In a setting, so divine!
That ease imagine how once lived
The great of nation, they so grand,
In such luxury, all hard earned,
Those who carved our future land,
One renowned for natural beauty,
Where Palace rest, seek reward,
Some respite in such splendour,
With Rose Gardens, rich award!

A gift to Duke, recognition,
Blenheim Palace in such a setting,
From grateful nation for his valour
When battle won, n'er forgetting
Name of place where battle fought,
Reason Palace itself was named,
When England beat the French in 1704
Reason ages, justly famed!
For England ever, grateful race,
Never sparing in our praise,
Thus great heroes we reward,
Draw on talent names we raise
To splendid heights, known all time,
With monuments, statues, this great house,
For Blenheim Palace such a mansion
Where our voice hear e'er roused,
Reflect scenic beauty, place of wonder,
See expense there, none see spared,
That all time Malborough, be remembered,
Etched for ever, great name repair!

C

The Orangery   Blenheim Palace

Used as a picture gallery by the 1st Duke, the Orangery which overlooks the Italian Gardens has been luxuriously refurbished as a banqueting and function suite. The same building was also used as a theatre by the 4th Duke where imagination tells us that many fine performances must have been performed there in the heyday of the Marlboroughs of the time.

That wonder not, Churchill's fame,
With such lineage, historic past,
Where ancient warriors come to mind,
Place his birthplace, this forecast
Great wartime leader, modern times,
For here it was he took first breath,
And like great ancestor, equal great,
Is remembered aft his death!
For known keen gardener, painting loved,
That seems the Palace had inspired
Winston Churchill in his youth,
Who true greatness did aspire,
And like the Duke, won great battle,
Showing tyrant England's door,
Recalls how Marlborough, that great Duke,
Winston, young, may have adored,
For here at Blenheim, Churchiliana seen,
Where simple room found, there the core,
Hallowed place, invite come worship,
There where Winston born in 1874.

London Our Heritage

Palaces and Towers, Castles and Kings,
London a showcase, hear the bells ring,
Brimming with history, all time has wrought,
With monuments standing, o'er ages bought;
As churches found where rise great spires,
That wonder such beauty, how minds inquire,
When St Paul's Cathedral, all view the dome,
Wren's masterpiece, a place all glad roam;
Where Baroque splendour, see symbol of State,
Great home religion, n'er known forsake,
With contrasts these many, view Carnaby Street,
Stroll there midst crowds, place there friends greet,
With alleyways branching, all find surprise,
See the Great Frog where baubles the prize,
This above pit where plague victims lie,
Their bones once found scattered near site where they died!

Close Regent Street where fashion has flourished,
See wealth incline, all this found nourished
Once where past dandies made their parade,
Find stylish folk stroll, place there still trade,
For street known a Makkah, where wish be seen
With elegant ladies, glad there they've been,
Viewed Regent Street, a crescent well known,
With curving edifice, place fashion grown;
All leading downstream, there found a land,
Theatres all leading to nightlife known grand!
Attracting the tourists and own kin too,
That wish from life's burden, escape not a few,
Though witness the traffic, crawling snail paced,
Through busy thoroughfares, for no place this race
As buses and cars, trail nose to nose,
That quicker to walk when congestion there grows!

Whilst shoppers and walkers, all make their way,
They keeping rules, keep cars at bay,
For not easy here, argue with stream
As seen traffic moving, all as a team,
Where places of culture too, these all may find,
As South Bank Centre, this springs to mind,
Lovers of Opera too, hear loved works grand,
For City of Music this, greatest in land,
Where at the Tate, Cézanne draws crowds,
Great genius on canvas, great artist proud,
As pastoral idyll 'Large Bathers' admire,
Such labour spent, find figures inspire,
As viewed the works, contours keen drawn,
Their presence echoes reflections few mourn,
Climactic canvas, drawn year artist's death,
Great final flourish, drawn 'fore last breath!

That visual art thus, London draws crowds,
When viewing artists, displayed all so proud,
Near highlight of City, there found 'Square Mile'
Where Stock Exchange, some there may smile,
Regular traders, working fixed rules,
For no place here harbour, financial fools,
Where Royal Courts of Justice too, these all come to view,
Place crimes are pondered, none known a few!
Near site all enter, Trafalgar Square,
See Column standing, see Nelson dare,
Blind eye to City turned, hero admire,
Great naval warrior, stout heart afire,
Proud heart defiant, towers o'er land saved,
Land from a tyrant, we n'er enslaved,
For ever thus, the British race,
Finds man of hour, one known keep face!

Oban

Oban, small town on Firth of Lorne,
Rare forsaken, none e'er mourn,
A small resort known Scottish lore
Near Isle of Mull, place adore,
Western Scotland, this the landscape,
Where life's troubles may escape,
Springboard for the Western Isles,
Place where seen there many smiles
Where sense to be, taking rest,
Reflecting ever life's great test,
For invigorating, bracing, take the air,
Away from City, wander there;
Reason inspiration there is found,
Composers writing works profound,
Joyous music, all inspired,
Poets too, all aspire
Reflect the spirit they all felt,
Fostered by the native Celt,
A hardy race, this dour but kind,
Solicitude ever, theirs we mind!

For there on honeymoon I there once
Tried wedded bliss, tried ensconce,
Arriving same day as the Queen,
Who Oban visited, and by all was seen,
That day remembered, heavens opened up
When heavy rain began to drop,
Lasted week, this I recall,
In mid-August, cast a pall
O'er the town, dampening air,
Dampened wish, stand and stare,
Despite event, bunting flapping,
Whilst 'gainst shore, waves were lapping,
Wettest month, known there for years,
Flooded streets, adding fears,
This an ill omen, happy trip,
Left feeling many a slip twixt cup and lip
As on quayside, the Queen alighted
When heavens opened, all seemed blighted,
With flags and bunting limply lying,
Leaving Oban sadly sighing!

This mainland town, a hilly region,
Where hikers, tourists, visit legion,
Loving all they such a landscape,
Find life's problems, brief escape,
Idyllic spot, town and sea,
Both together, great feel free
As sailing, bathing, all take choice
When beauty seen, all rejoice;
With Buchan's country, this so near,
Makes setting for his works seem clear,
Remote and wild, such resort,
Many finding place for sport,
That Oban known an ideal town,
For no place this, a place to frown,
Though Baron Tweedsmuir n'er did name
In his novels, Oban's fame,
But atmosphere in books be found,
Same as Oban, look around,
Found perfect setting for such plots
That pity author n'er wrote lots!

Westminster Abbey

Architectural masterpiece, stands the Abbey,
Central Church, great in land,
Presenting pageant of British history
Throughout the centuries, all so grand!
Where here found countless memorials,
These to great and good and famed,
Where seen the tombs of many Kings,
All too numerous here to name!
Place Coronations have their setting,
A Royal event, revered all time,
As other chapters in British history,
Here main Church, adore, divine!
Where found marble effigies of past Monarchs,
With Elizabeth I Tudor Queen,
O'er same vault where lies half-sister,
Mary Tudor, Monarch been!
Both lie in glory Henry VII's Chapel,
Seen outstanding Tudor style,
With vaulted roof seen coloured banners,
Gaze in wonder, queue a mile!

        Marvel Chapel, Edward the Confessor,
        Abbey's founder, saintly King,
        When consecrated in eleventh century,
        Bells of mourning soon heard ring,
        For some days later came the news,
        Edward he himself, had died,
        For seems his own tomb he had built
        Within the Abbey, there to lie!
        Where near his shrine, five Kings, four Queens,
        Worthy Church all lie today,
        After Henry III had rebuilt
        This great Abbey, meant to stay!
        Where is seen the Coronation Chair,
        Designed to hold famed great stone,
        Seized from Scots in thirteenth century,
        Once itself derived from Scone!
        And for the Coronation, Chair moved to Sanctuary
        Where each Monarch there is crowned,
        Great event seen Lords and Ladies,
        In attendance, richly gowned!

Westminster Abbey

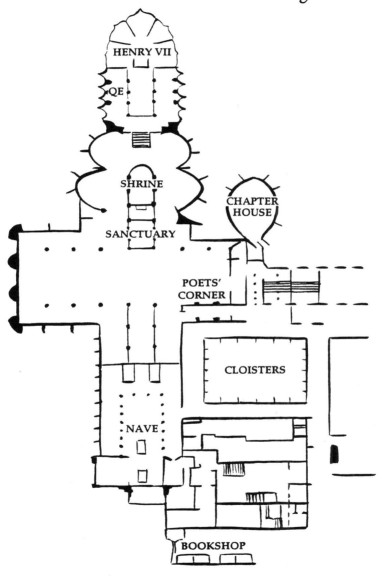

For here the focal point of Abbey,
Where may view medieval art,
Masterpieces all of Italian Renaissance,
That how view all, wonder start?
With Poets' Corner, inspired by Chaucer,
Poet noted for his narrative skill,
Humour, wit, prerequisites
With sense of rhythm, nothing still!
For this great founder lies in Abbey,
First great poet in the land,
Lying in imposing tomb,
Time n'er ending n'er the sand,
Place here memorial to all great poets,
See full-length statue of Shakespeare,
Carved one century after death,
He did at last to all appear;
Who great bard, nation's heritage
With other poets, find enshrined,
Auden, Thomas and Lewis Carroll,
Find their memorials, all great minds!

New Place/Nash's House

The site and foundations of New Place, in Shakespeare's day a large and handsome house where he spent his retirement and died in 1616, were purchased for preservation in 1862. The site on the corner of Chapel Street, opposite the historic Guild Chapel, is presented as a garden and an Elizabethan-style knot garden is a special feature. Entry is through the adjoining Nash's House which belonged to Thomas Nash, the first husband of Shakespeare's granddaughter, Elizabeth Hall.

Nash House has a Tudor interior with period furnishings together with local archaeological and historic material illustrating the earlier and later history of Stratford.

Greenwich

Greenwich, centre, time and space,
Maritime history, hard keep pace,
Developments made these o'er the years,
Read naval history, allay all fears,
Built in setting near Greenwich Park,
With bustling town near, see history stark,
Where old buildings, shops abound,
Curious folk wish look around,
See listed buildings, one Queen's House,
Architectural masterpiece, does arouse
Interested folk come see and wonder,
Timeless elegance, here may ponder
Such a building, pure display,
Marvel splendour, no affray,
With tranquil beauty, all serene,
Glad to see, glad have been
Viewed the house with historic landscape,
Where no wish here, e'er escape,
Such a building, classic style,
All glad examine, travel miles!

And see Museum, Britannia's Glory,
Where let naval history tell own story,
How maritime power it aims defend
Our great land, so fences mend!
And October, see large display
About great hero, man his day,
Recall Trafalgar, mourn the death
When Nelson battling took last breath;
Legend he in own lifetime,
N'er letting enemy cross the line,
Endanger nation, freedom lost,
Fighting right when lives it cost,
Remembered all time, great sea fight,
When Great Britain retained its might;
Recalled with monument seen Trafalgar Square,
Climb great height, ask who dares!
Not high enough for this great man,
For naval crew, they prove a clan,
Where Greenwich too is such a place,
Recall with pride how defend our race!

Tragic stories too remind
Where *Titanic* divers too may find
Many objects brought from wreck,
Where once folk they walked on deck,
On greatest liner, all time known,
How it sank, divers shown,
Two miles down in icy sea,
Death so sudden, showed little mercy,
Hear how boat it hit the ice,
Tore great hole where death played dice,
When many souls were lost that day,
Gave little chance there fear allay,
All those waiting on the shore,
Those beloved, see no more,
For unsinkable, *Titanic* claimed,
Tragic memory recalls the name,
Hear at Greenwich past great dream
For famed *Titanic*, named had been,
But now from depths of ocean, relics brought,
To surface land in danger sought!

That now at Greenwich, much remind,
Naval memories, many find,
All hands gallery, here approach,
Historic past, none reproach,
For Britain known great naval power,
Where historic acts, tales here tower,
In twentieth century, aim defend,
Place where folk memorabilia lend,
Models, pictures show sea trade,
Pirates never, none e'er raid,
For fine tradition, great sea wars,
Where life at sea is known own law,
Where much at Greenwich here relate
Of Captain Cook so much narrate,
How nation's boundaries helped extend,
Updated gallery, seen much lent,
Adds to knowledge much sea lore,
Leaves men wishing they hear more,
Greatest legends ever told,
Of naval heroes, English bold!

Cutty Sark

A three-masted merchant clipper built in 1869, now kept at Greenwich
London [named after the witch in Robert Burns' poem Tam o'Shanter
who wore only a cutty sark (short shirt)].

A Rural Idyll

Fields and hedgerows, nature's quilt,
See rural England, perceptive built,
A sprawling landscape, undulating,
In our clime seen formulating,
Such a bedspread, where seen graze,
Cattle they in nature's maze!
A complex labyrinth, spanning land,
Hedge divided, fields see manned,
Cultivated they with loving care,
Makes beauteous sight, a pattern rare,
Where crops are tilled, all these with thought,
Rhythmic seasons, leaving nought,
N'er to chance as toil required,
So fruit of labour may acquire
Crown our work with rich rewards,
Thus harvest fruit, enjoy awards!

Makkah, central towns these stand,
View squares and buildings, hallowed land,
Where farmers they may others meet,
Rural folk there, weekly greet,
As village life, outskirts around,
Centuries old, these abound!
Witness Hereford, foremost mind,
With Weobley close, quaint reminds,
Times forgotten, recalls the past,
As Elizabethan dwellings, long seen last,
Where live sleepy, rustic folk,
They all thriving, tied to yoke,
Unwilling face the present date,
Recall past tales, these still relate,
Reflect the charm theirs, country life,
As try forget they modern strife!

See leafy Warwickshire, lovely place,
Tucked away, seek other face,
Where mansions lie, see Newbold Revel,
A lovely house built, land seen level,
Where on the lake seen proud swans glide,
Midst water lilies, trees' shade hide,
Whilst sumptuous fountain plays on lawn,
There where goldfish too may spawn,
They their eggs, offspring offer
Ensuring next year all may proffer
Glittering fish seen darting swift,
That these when viewed feel spirits lift,
As seen beyond, rich arable land,
Fertile, fruitful, vista grand,
Lending grace to mansion fine,
With great edifice, stands refined!

But countryside moves slower pace,
As time stands still with no sense race,
When little change seen, colours mellow,
As leaves they turn from green to yellow;
For seems the trees are nature's clock,
As view these changes, men take stock,
When movement slow whilst corn turns gold,
When ready reap e'er harvest old,
Whilst sheep and cattle, they move slow,
No sense hasten, though time flows,
Where all moves rhythmic, even, steady,
Though much swift when winter ready,
As cattle refuge take in barns,
When men find time exchanging yarns,
Relate their progress made through year,
With work complete, trust nothing fear!

Hampton Court Palace

Jewel in the Crown, Hampton Court stands,
Palace to Kings lies here on our land,
Tranquil the setting, there by the Bank,
Next River Thames, Royal heritage flanks!
Ancient Royal home for four hundred years
Where once was heard laughter whilst others shed tears!
History repeating events behind these walls
Where for each Monarch, time n'er let pall.
As walk through each room see how all once lived,
Leaves an impression, richness all gives,
With sumptuous paintings, Renaissance the style,
Furnishings too see, mile upon mile!
Rich tapestry of history, Tudor, Baroque,
With restored Privy Garden, seen stroll many folk!
View Henry VIII's Apartments, sense atmosphere,
For remembered this Monarch, one greatly feared!
With Great Hall and Chape recalling his time,
Seen all in keeping, this Tudor line!
For here in the Palace, each Monarch left mark,
Brilliant, outstanding, splendour stands stark!
As through King's Apartments seen painted by hand,
Stairs these so regal, magnificence stands,
For rife throughout Palace, history alive,
Where events here remembered, greatness see strive,
As wandering freely, all sense an awe,
Great monument to past, behind each great door!
That grandeur this scale, n'er been surpassed,
This mirror to history where peer into glass,
All time remembered recall we this scene,
Great Tudor Palace which beckons be seen!

Hampton Court Palace

Leafy Pinner

Leafy Pinner, quaint delight,
Dainty village, black and white,
Adorns Home Counties, workers' dreamscape,
Place pleased sleep and then awake,
For rustic life here, out of town,
Giving few a reason frown,
Since quiet contentment here found rests,
A townsfolk's respite, magic nest
As seen the High Street with olde worlde charm,
No place to fear or feel alarm,
For back in time seen little change,
With ease uncover history's range,
Since not unknown found centuries old,
A house off beat where seen Priest's hole,
With cunning panels, so disguising
A hideaway, today surprising,
Ingenious means found Henry's time,
Camouflaging site seen all in line,
Where in secret, mass once said,
A place where *"Ite, missa est"* was read!

A new Catholic Church though now we find,
Down Love Lane where seen enshrined
A modern building with fine view,
Proud, throwing light, seen different, new,
With architecture planned in present age,
Forward looking, all the rage,
Standing there on same ground
Where older Church too may be found,
Comparison diminutive, looking small,
Though past history, nothing palls
Where other Churches nearby stand,
Go up the High Street, find prime land,
Corner Paines Lane, old church seen,
This a gem 'tis easy glean,
Focal point of village life,
Place withstanding urban strife,
With grey stone Church, featuring clock tower,
Place to meet, sense village power
Where pious folk there all glad greet,
They each other, place all meet!

Seems Pinner Toy Town, 'tis neat place,
With Waxwell Lane see other face,
As seen the Police Station there at top,
Near old cottages, quaint, we stop,
Where opposite Station, country pub,
Neighbours, drinkers, there's the rub!
Seems all so friendly, wonder crime,
And in this age, we wonder rhyme?
That no surprise here homes much sought,
Where found antique shops, where much is bought,
For all so charming seen the High Street
Where seek hostelries, good food eat,
That wonder not, live here the famed,
Living hopeful, free from strain,
For easy avenue, dreamy landscape,
Tranquil suburb gives time escape,
Where able shut day on tomorrow,
These too many, hope few follow,
As leave the world by turning key,
Wish shut out past, to Pinner flee!

Kew

Come to Kew, see tranquil gardens
Where earth's environment strives conserve
A lovely place, there may see,
We earth's splendour, men deserve;
Where such beauty there find thriving
In lilac time, all glad come view
Exotic blooms, grown abundant,
Place to visit, come to Kew!
For world famed here see stunning gardens,
Ask where begin, make request,
As unabated, grown through year,
Lovely flowers, rejoice bequest,
Glad such gardens find world famed,
They unrivalled, they elsewhere,
All see thrive in spectacular houses
Where men gaze, come and stare
When no other exhibits such as these
May view together, such collection,
Makes memorable visits, those who come,
Glad later years, makes recollection!

For lovely plants found here unique,
All manner of flora, Kew embrace,
Where winter too seen stunning gardens,
Colourful pageant, origin trace,
Near the Thames, there at Richmond
That seek location, find the place,
Close to heaven, untold splendour
Which our country, gardens grace!
For rich diversity, here encompass
Formal gardens with natural woodland,
Wetland fields too seen with the meadows,
Adds to interest, all seems grand!
Place of wonder, how all marvel
With so much see throughout the year,
With changing seasons, all reflected,
See rotations, nought here fear,
For natural beauty find so calming,
Illumines wonders held in soil,
Where found cradle here to seedlings,
That rare find reason growth may foil!

For gift to nation, famous gardens,
Welcomed first in Victoria's reign,
Just one century since men forecast
How future unfolds, nought here feigned,
For society then held up to scrutiny,
Naturalists, scientists, they foresaw
Rapid growth, inventive minds,
That study flora, all adore!
A place which Wordsworth would have loved
When Lake District saw daffodils rest heads on stones,
Along the shores of Lake Ullswater,
Translated Kew too, there seen grow,
Flowers known, they Lent Lilies,
All synonymous with the spring,
Whose yellow bell heads all see shake,
Transferred to Kew, hear them ring!
Narcissus pseudonarcissus, bordering Lakes,
Inspired the poet, he to write
Of flowers enjoyed, tossing their heads,
In town setting, all upright!

Josiah Wedgwood

Josiah Wedgwood, British potter,
Raised his craft of unique blue hue
With design of subtle beauty
to classic art, raised Wedgwood Blue,
Seen artefacts all, inspired two centuries,
Major products, these supreme,
Makes Stoke-on-Trent, where all crafted,
Place of pilgrimage, glad all been;
Where urns and vases, *objets d'art*,
Seem inspired, some teal green,
With varied shapes of Grecian beauty,
Makes all marvel see Grecian scenes;
Noble figures, some with horses,
Décor white 'gainst blue background,
Every scene with care find spaced,
Examine close as turn around,
For breathtaking, lovely objects,
That wonder not, feel no distaste
For such perfection, British craft,
Pure and lovely, all so chaste!

For past patrons, Queen Charlotte
Commissioned service, known Queen's Ware,
The name still carried to this day,
That argue else, advise beware!
Josiah inspiring he perfection,
Worked with finest artists known his day,
With Stubbs and Flaxman, these included,
Their commitment led the way,
Set a standard 'gainst which others measured,
Lent a lustre, to Wedgwood's name
Which today has never faded,
Pleasing all who purchased fame,
With tableware, rooted history,
As artistry echoed in cream coloured ware,
That argue else is a fool's game,
As only this, just fools would dare,
Remembering Josiah Wedgwood "Father of English Potters"
He ceramics offered new designs,
Alternative to the rest of Europe,
For Wedgwood he n'er know resign!

With ease imagine Collectors' haven,
With varied function, every piece,
As objects linked by many factors
With material factors, much released!
For all such ranges give much pleasure,
All so many, great the choice,
With plates and vases and small boxes,
See Christmas ware, glad rejoice!
With gold edged linings, Avebury enchances,
Seen sumptuous russet and red rose,
Softened all by trailing foliage,
Collectors' items, those who know;
For every item, care is crafted,
Wedgwood adding ever range,
Nostalgic Kutani Crane looks back
To Victoria, e'er came change,
Though forward image, Countryware
Assures us all alive today
That town and country are united
Through Josiah Wedgwood, showing way!